Workington in old picture postcards volume 1

by
D. Woodruff
and
K. Walker

European Library – Zaltbommel/Netherlands

A nostalgic look at Old Workington with photographs selected and compiled by Messrs. D. Woodruff and K. Walker.

Through the services of the Carnegie Centre, Workington, the compilers of this volume are currently recording the local heritage by the copying of old postcards and photographs of local historical interest.
Acknowledgements for help received must go to The Workington Historical Society, Workington Library, The Helena Thompson Museum and especially to all those individuals who have allowed us the use of their photographs and knowledge.

Second edition: 1993

GB ISBN 90 288 3497 4 / CIP

INTRODUCTION

The town of Workington is situated on the west coast of Cumbria, south of Carlisle and across the Solway Firth from Scotland. For the past few centuries now, it has derived its living from coal, heavy industries, especially those of steel making and farming. As a market town it is situated on the southern side of the River Derwent, the town proper overlooking the river from a raised position. Around the River Mouth as it enters the sea are centred the Docks and the Marsh and Quay areas. On high ground, about a mile and a quarter inland stand the ruins of Workington Hall, once the seat of the Curwens, Lords of the Manor of Workington.

The town has a long history reaching back to the Roman occupation. On the north side of the river was built the Roman Fort of Gabresentum. Excavations there unearthed pottery of the Hadrianic Period showing the fort to have been part of the coastal defences. It was the Angles, who gave the town its name, Wyrekington (the Inga Tun or settlement of Weorca, or possibly Wyre, meaning river) during the 7th century. Built into the fabric of St. Michael's Parish Church, were found remnants of Anglo-Saxon crosses.

In the 11th century the town was possessed by the Normans during their invasion of the northern Shires. Ketel, grandson of Ivo de Tailbois (who came to England with the Conqueror) had two sons. Orme, the younger, in marrying the sister of the First Lord of Allerdale, received the Manor of Seaton and built his keep on the site of the old Roman Fort. His grandson, Thomas, brought into the family the name de Culwen (or Curwen as it became) and it was his son Patric de Culwen who, in the 13th century, moved to the high ground on the south side of the river, and there built his residence (the Hall) with the town progressing around this. Workington has been the centre of steel making in north-west England for over a hundred years. Railway lines have been exported all over the world from her plants. In 1883 Charles Cammell and company removed the Dronfield Works from Sheffield and set them up in Workington. With them came practically an entire community. Many a Workingtonian can claim a 'Dronie' ancestry. It was the death of a Yorkshire town but the start of a Cumbrian industrial empire. Seaton Ironworks changed to the manufacture of tin plate. Its workers being imported from a Welsh community not only brought Workington an extra industry but an annual Music Festival, which is still enjoyed today. There were two shipbuilding yards together with a ropery and saw mills. The 244th and last ship to be built was launched in 1938.

With the coming of the Railways, Workington continued to expand. A report from 1912 tells us that the town possessed: Two Protestant Episcopal Churches, St. Michael's Parish Church and St. John's Church, and one Chapel of Ease. St. Mary's Church, Westfield and Christ Church. The Roman Catholic Church, the Presbyterian, Congregational, Wesleyan Methodist, Primitive Methodist, Baptist and United Methodist Churches. There are also the Wesleyan Methodist Mission Halls in Queen Street and Westfield, the Central Hall, the Gospel Hall, Salvation Mission Hall, Seaman's Bethel and Salvation Army Barracks.

The public buildings include the various Council Schools, Police Station, public covered market, four banks, the

Drill Hall, Albert Hall, Public Hall, the Carnegie Free Library, Reading Room and Hall, Queens Opera House, Theatre, the Savings Bank, Dispensary, the Infirmary, Auction Mart and so on, that gives a picture of a thriving market town with its roots buried in the past.

Together with Workington, can be found the small township of Harrington, whose history and progress are linked and intertwined. Harrington over the years possessing an industrial heritage that has formed part of Workington's past.

Workington played its part in the history of the region throughout the years. The Curwens were involved in the Border Wars with Scotland. Various Curwens, Sir Gilbert II and later Sir Gilbert III fought against such Scots heroes as Wallace, Bruce and Sir James Douglas. They were involved with De Harcla when he made peace with Bruce, King of the Scots. For this De Harcla was condemned as a traitor and lost his life. The Curwens lost their lands, only to have them restored shortly afterwards in 1329. The first person to write of Workington was Lelend, Chaplain to Henry VIII, who describes the town as 'Where ships come to where there is a pretty fisher town called Wyrekington and there is the chief house of Sir Thomas Curwen'. In 1568 Mary Queen of Scots, fleeing from the lost battle of Langside arrived by boat at Workington and was received by Sir Henry Curwen who provided her with food and shelter, escorting her to Cockermouth and from there Mary continued along the journey that was to end with the executioners axe.

It was in 1573 that a Charter was granted to Workington to hold a market and fair. From thence market days have been every Wednesday and Saturday. For a number of years cattle auctions were held in Guard Street. Fairs are generally held at Whitsuntide and in October.

Thomas Pennant, the historian visiting Cumberland in 1774, describes Workington as 'Extending from the sea to the castle, with the inhabitants subsisting by the coal trade'.

William Hutchinson, writing in 1794 states: *The increase of this place has been very rapid and many of the new buildings are handsome; the town containing up to 1,200 houses. There are now 160 vessels in this port, the chief trade is in coal for Ireland. The imports are timber and ship building materials. The number of inhabitants is computed at 6,000. The lower part of the town is on a marsh, hence the name of Marsh Side and Quay.*

The progress of the town can be dated from here-on. Coal was of great importance to industry and during the 18th and 19th centuries over thirty pits were open at various dates. The Port of Workington too progressed with this trade. Regarded as a safe harbour with breakwater and quays it was created an Independent Port in 1850 and later in 1917 a concrete pier 1,000 feet in length was built.

Following the introduction of steelmaking on nearby sites a large dock was created in 1865 and named after Lord Lonsdale. This dock was later widened and deepened to take ships of some 10,000 tons. Renamed the Prince of Wales Dock it was opened by His Royal Highness in June 1927.

1. *The Parish Church of St. Michael's.* There has been a church on this site, originating from the 7th century, as shown by the finding of Saxon cross fragments which had been built into the Norman all stone edifice. Built during the 12th century this fabric stood up until the year of 1770 when it was replaced by a much larger erection. Unfortunately a severe fire in January 1887 completely destroyed the interior of the building and services had to be suspended for about three years. The present edifice dates from 1890 and is of freestone with sandstone facings. The interior contains chancel, nave and aisles. The porch faces south-west and a tall clock tower exhibits a clock and contains eight bells, which are rung regularly. Inside the church one can find mementos of the Curwen family and the board recording past Rectors and Ministers includes the name of Wordsworth, one of the sons of the poet W. Wordsworth, who in marrying a Curwen heiress enjoyed the living of the church for a period.

2. *Workington Hall.* This hereditary seat of the Curwen's was created when Patric de Culwen moved from his tower on the north side of the River Derwent to this present site overlooking the south bank. The Hall has been in continuous occupation up until 1939, when it was presented to the local council. The first all stone building of a Pele tower was erected by Sir Gilbert III in 1362 during the period of the Scottish Wars. The first hall at ground level was built in 1404. Added to in 1538 and later, by 1610 this border fortress was transformed into a Tudor Mansion. The original Pele tower being incorporated into the general design. It was in 1568 that Mary, Queen of Scots, sought shelter as a fugitive. The Curwens brought about many improvements in the life of the town. John Christian Curwen, in the 19th century, owned a number of mines and the estate farm of Schoose. Through the mines and other interests he brought about a form of social security. On the payment of a few pence a week, extracted from his workers wages, those self same workers received compensation, when they were ill, suffered accidents, and in the case of death the funeral expenses were catered for. He was an innovator in the field of agriculture. Not only did his experiments increase his crop yields, but these were passed on to his workers in the form of lower priced vegetables etc.

3. *The Hall Mill, Millfield, circa 1920.* There has been a corn mill on this site for centuries. Every Feudal Estate had its mill and Workington is no exception. There is no date for this present building, but it is reputed to be about 300 years old. In the early years of this century it has been used as a saw mill. In its day it was water driven, the wheel still in evidence in the 1930's. It was fed by a mill race taken from the River Derwent which flows nearby. This stream re-enters the River Derwent under Workington Bridge. The Millfields themselves are a popular area for courting couples and Sunday strollers. They are also used as the venue for Agricultural Shows and other outdoor sports and leisure activities.

4. *The Yearl in Millfield, circa 1900.* The Yearl is a weir and fish trap on the River Derwent. For centuries this has been the scene of a salmon fishery held by the Curwens. In spring it is a common sight to see salmon swimming upstream to spawn in the upper reaches of the river. In the 19th century the opposite bank of the river had a small iron works, The Seaton Iron Works. One of the products was cannon. These were test fired by shooting cannon balls across the river into the steep banking on the south side. In hot summers the weir was also the scene of swimming, providing as it did a deep calm pool.

5. *Workington Harbour, 1900.* In the reign of Henry VIII, Workington was described as a 'pretty little fisher town'. In 1590 there were only ten vessels in all of Cumberland. By 1882, 117 ships used Workington Harbour alone. This had been preceded by the building of the Lonsdale Dock in 1865. The growth of mining and the production of iron and steel in the early 1900's led to the widening and deepening of the harbour and the erection of the Prince of Wales Dock in 1927. Under the auspices of a free harbour, vessels sheltering in the dock because of adverse weather conditions were exempt from duties. From 22nd June 1869, local fishing boats were ordered to distinguish themselves by displaying the letters W.O. on their sides in large lettering. The main trade of the port in those days was pig iron, steel rails, iron ore, timber and coal to Ireland.

6. *Hagg Hill Market, circa 1910.* This twice weekly open air market originated from the granting of a Charter in 1573. It was held at the upper end of the town where there is also a covered market but in the early years of this century removed to the lower end of the town here at Hagg Hill. To the side of the market is an arcade and in the left hand corner is to seen a cast iron urinal, a common site in the Victorian era.

7. *Schoose Farm.* This was the estate farm run by the Curwen family. It was complete with its own windmill and here J.C. Curwen in the 19th century experimented with increasing his crop yield and by introducing European grasses with which to feed his dairy herd also doubled his milk production. He was a great innovator in the field of agriculture, not only winning for himself gold awards but introducing into the town the custom of holding annual cattle shows and the like.

8. *Cuckoo Arch, 1910.* Schoose Farm lies east of the Workington Hall estate across a valley which carries the main road. In order to link the two parts of the estate Sir Henry Curwen in the mid-19th century, caused this arch to be built. Over the years it reached the status of a local monument. The Lowther family from Penrith, who owned land in the district, were regarded as the rivals to the Curwens, the two factions often being on opposite sides in political arguments of the era. It was often said that the arch was built so that should the Lowthers have to pass under it in their carriage the Curwens up above could spit upon it or rain down stones. The arch was destroyed in October 1931.

9. *Billy Bumbly House, 1910.* This was another famous landmark of Workington. There were two of these built in the 19th century to be coastal landmarks as an aid to ships entering the harbour. One is positioned nearby to the harbour and this one a distance south of the harbour on the Shore Hills. Painted white their name arises because of their similarity to a beehive. Billy Bumbley being a local name for the bumble bee. Originally built with door and sea facing window for placing lights they were eventually filled in to make a solid structure.

10. *Billy Bumbley House.* Tide waiters or tide watchers were docks overseers with the duties of checking ships in and out of the harbour. Checking the ship's manifests, seeing that the cargoes were correctly loaded, helping out with the customs and excise in the search for contraband and generally administrating to the running of the docks. They lived in cottages on the shore and as the photograph shows this one lies just below The Billy Bumbley Landmark. Stories handed down have the cottages and their occupants in league with the smugglers that at one time infested this west coast region.

11. *The Catholic Mission circa 1900.* In 1811 a monk of the Order of St. Benedict was appointed to the charge of a Mission in Workington owing to the large number of Irishmen here working as labourers etc. J.C. Curwen gave a site and the Mission and house for the priest as shown in the photograph were built soon after. In the background can be seen How Michael. This was a Chantry Chapel granted in the reign of Elizabeth I to Percy Gunson and John Soukey. Its conspicuous position makes it a landmark for Mariners and in the early years of this century it was used as a magazine and battery by the locally raised Artillery Company.

12. *The Catholic Church of Our Lady and St. Michael's.* The large influx of Irishmen to work in the steel works, made it necessary to have a larger church. Reverend C.W. Clifton who was then in charge of the Mission at Chapel Bank exerted himself successfully in the matter. The present church was opened for worship in 1876 and has seating accommodation for over 800. The total cost of the building and its surroundings amounted to £11,000. The style is early English and the interior consists of transepts, nave, aisles, chancel and there are a number of very fine stained glass windows.

13. *St. John's Church.* This was erected in 1823 as a celebration of the Battle of Waterloo. It has a portico of the Doric style supported by four massive pillars. It is supposed to resemble the Church of St. Paul at Covent Garden, London. By the passing of an Ecclesiastical Act in 1856, St. John's is for all purposes a separate and distinct parish. During the time of the cholera in the 1850's, the churchyard was enlarged to its present size, but like St. Michael's, since the opening of the Harrington Road Cemetery only those who have relatives buried in the churchyard are now interred here.

14. *The Baptist Church, Harrington Road, 1910.* The Baptist following in Workington was formed as a branch of Maryport, worship taking place in rooms in Edkin Street. After fruitless efforts members of the church were able to form a separate body of Workington Baptists. The foundation stones of the church were laid in 1886 and the church opened for worship in September of that same year. But it was not until 1st March 1888 that the Workington Baptists were able to assume a separate entity.

15. *Cross Hill about 1910.* Cross Hill stands on the main road leading out of town in the upper part of the town itself. In the middle ages, St. Michael's, the Parish Church, did not have any rights of Internment, so funerals had to pass through the town, ford the river and go on to Camerton for the burial. Here at Cross Hill was a small Chapel of Ease, where the party could rest the coffin and have a homily read over the deceased. Built into the walls of one of the houses are two carved stone crosses. Records show that the chapel was rebuilt during the reign of Richard II. In the early 1900's one of the residents of Cross Hill was a Mr. Bacon... a butcher.

16. *Guard Street School, 1912.* This School of Industry was established in 1816 to 'provide for the instruction of Young Ladies to make them notable housekeepers and good christians'. It later developed into the 'Higher Grade School', the whole of the technical instruction, science and art, and manual subjects being under the control of a committee, consisting of members of the Town Board and Town Council. It also held a Pupil Teacher's Centre, under control of the same Board.

17. *Technical College, circa 1920.* The College was opened in 1912 and contained a Secondary School for Boys and Girls, a Junior Technical School, a Technical Institute for Post Matriculation Studies, together with day and afternoon classes, also evening classes. The school was eventually recognised by the Education Authorities as a local college, providing for both major and minor scholarships. During its years as a school it was controlled by a board of 12 governers. Today, much enlarged and modernised, it is the West Cumbria College.

18. *The Carnegie Free Library and Hall, 1910.* The Library and Lecture Hall was erected by 1904 under a grant of £7,500 from the Trust of Andrew Carnegie of Skibo Castle. The previous library had been housed in the premises of the Savings Bank on Pow Street since 1891. The stock of over 22,500 books being transferred. To obtain a book you handed in your request to the clerk, who then searched for it, and then booked it out. Over the years the Lecture Hall has been used as a theatre and picture palace.

19. *Finkle Street before 1900.* This photograph shows Finkle Street before the erection of the Carnegie Building (on the left). The church in the distance is the Trinity Methodist Church which was built in 1890 to replace one that had been burned down in 1889. Designed in the Italian style it contained a Sunday School of six classrooms, lecture hall and kitchen on the ground floor. On the upper floor were to be found a large schoolroom and a library.

20. *Harrington Road, 1904.* This photograph shows the junction of Vulcan's Lane with Harrington Road. In the centre of the road stands what was a common sight in the Victorian era, a cast iron urinal. This one had the nickname of 'St. Paul's, due no doubt to its domed roof. The gable end of the house bears several advertisements and to its immediate left is a Monumental Masons. Across the road from here and to the right of the picture are the gates of Workington Cemetery.

21. *Laying the foundation stone of Workington Hospital in August 1885.* The stone laying ceremony was attended by civic dignitaries and as the photograph shows by the various church groups and other banner carrying associations for this, the first purpose built hospital in the town, was paid for by the townspeople themselves. The extremely large sum of over £2,736 needed to complete the building was raised entirely through voluntary contributions. The running costs for the next 62 years were also met by the local population.

22. *Workington Hospital circa 1912.* In return for the promise of medical care, workers at the steel works contributed 1d a week out of their wages and as late as 1927 these workers contributions met fifty per cent of the infirmary's costs. Not all could take advantage of the facilities. The rules at the time stated: 'People suffering from mania (madness), epilepsy, contagious, infectious, chronic, or incurable diseases,' would be barred from entry. Without these exceptions the infirmary would have been unable to cope with the demand because in 1888 with a local population of 24,000 the hospital only had 16 beds. Is it irony or just the siting of the hospital to be just behind the cemetery?

23. *Workington Fever Hospital 1904.* Built in the 19th century to the east of the town the building originally was intended to house unfortunates. Known generally as the Poor House it in fact saw very few paupers. Some of the people who resided there actually supported themselves and on occasions the governing body found themselves making a profit. As the Fever Hospital it took those infectious and contagious diseases that the Infirmary refused.

24. *The local coach service, circa 1890.* During the latter years of the 19th century and the early years of the 20th century, Mr. W. Smith, landlord of the Lowther Arms Hotel in Portland Street, ran a twice weekly coach service between the town and Moss Bay on market days. The coach was driven by his son John, shown here collecting passengers on Nook Street.

25. *Derwent Engineering Company 1908.* Situated on Central Square, the Derwent Engineering Co. were the town's motor experts in those early days of motoring. This corner of John Street and Central Square has changed very little for there is still a garage and showroom here. Over the years only the motor experts and the models have changed.

26. *Workington's first commercial vehicle.* In 1910, Mr. Dunne, a garage proprietor had the distinction of what he claimed to be the first passenger car converted to the carrying of goods. Shown above it was a 'Globe' originally belonging to a Mr. Lister, furnisher of Finkle Street. It could do 'with luck' 30 miles an hour and consume 25 miles to the gallon and could be converted to carry livestock in the rear seats. Mr. Dunne had constructed a box which could replace the rear seats with room to carry half a dozen pigs. The car operates from a one cylinder, 10 H.P. engine.

27. *Bonnington's grocery van, circa 1920's.* W.E. Bonnington had a grocer's shop at 81 Harrington Road and delivered locally taking a selection of groceries around the outlying districts. His first delivery van was horse drawn but shown here is the van used in the 1920's dressed up for a Carnival Shopping Week.

28. *Gustave Hamel and his aeroplane, 1913.* For their annual sports day in 1913, Workington secured the visit of Gustave Hamel, who in April of that year had flown non stop between England and Germany. The aviator agreed to make several flights carrying a passenger free of charge each time. When Saturday 23rd August arrived more than 14,000 spectators turned up to witness the historic day. Unfortunately a strong gale (to which this coastline is frequently subjected), made it doubtful about the flights taking place. Hamel decided to go ahead but taking only his mechanic as passenger. The plane took off, flew a circuit but when attempting to land found that the press of people crowded the landing area in Lonsdale Park and the bad gales forced him out to sea where he ditched the plane into the water. He and his mechanic were able to wade ashore and members of the crowd assisted them to pull the machine to dry land.

29. *Station Road, 1910.* This view is looking down towards Low Station, which in the 1900's was the principle station for the London and North West Railway Company, with trains running north and south along the coast. The original station was built in the 1870's and due to the increased industrial traffic, goods yards were erected in 1881 and the passenger station was entirely rebuilt and enlarged about five years later. The station has remained more or less the same design since.

30. *Central Station circa 1930.* Up until the 1960's and the 'Beeching Axe', Workington had three railway stations. The Low Station, Workington Bridge Station and this, The Central Station. Sited in the centre of town on John Street and adjoining Central Square, it was the principal station of the Workington and Cleator Moor Railway, originally built as a mineral line. Today the site is taken over by a car park, which on Wednesdays and Saturdays holds the twice weekly open market.

31. *Workington Bridge Station, 1910.* This station was also rebuilt in 1881 and provided passengers with an entry into the heart of the Lake District via the Workington, Cockermouth, Keswick and Penrith Railway. It was a branch off the Low Station junction and also carried coal and coke for the use of the iron works.

32. Pow Street, 1910. Pow Street has long been Workington's main shopping area. Along this street were to be found butchers, bakers, banks, newsagents, shoe shops, tailors, and later came the chain stores of Woolworth's and Marks and Spencers. In the centre of the picture can be seen the arched entrance to the Opera House and opposite is Mandales Clock. Sited above the jewellers, this was the meeting place for young couples. 'See you under Mandales Clock,' was a common saying when making a date with someone.

33. *Pow Street, 1912.* This photograph is looking down Pow Street from the opposite end and down from the upper part of town. To the left is the Lowther Arms Hotel with its unusual turreted façade, and Eastman's the butcher on the opposite corner.

34. *McAleer the shoe shop, 1912.* As seen by the photograph, French and American boots stocked and you are invited to try his horseskin boots. His advertisement for this year of 1912 states that he has footwear up to date. He further goes on to say that great changes have taken place in the shapes and cut, by which a remarked improvement in appearance and greater comfort in wear are the appreciable outcome.

35. *Birkinshaw the tailors and outfitters, 1912.* Sited on the Market Square at Hag Hill was J. Birkinshaw, tailor and outfitter, always showing a choice selection of men's, youth's and juvenile clothing. In 1912 his sales included men's suits from 12/6, trousers from 2/11, youth's suits from 8/6, with good fit and good workmanship guaranteed.

36. *Workington Brewery, 1912.* Established in the 19th century under local ownership, this brewery stands to the rear of Pow Street on Ladies Walk and overlooking the River Derwent. It owned the majority of inns in the area and was well-known for the quality of its ales and beers.

37. *Jane Street, circa 1915.* Another shopping street, Jane Street boasted the Co-op building to the left and on the right Workington's noted hardware dealers, Scaifes. This particular view is looking up towards the bridge spanning the Central Station and railway and to the recently built Oxford Cinema.

38. *Washington Street, 1900.* On Washington Street could be found the smithy, The Old Crown and the New Crown Hotels, Workington Town Hall and the Theatre Royal. This was first opened in 1866, capable of seating 700 under the name of the Lyceum. Several businesses and shops are also to be found on this street.

39. *Palmer's Fish Shop, 1912.* One of the businesses to be found on Washington Street was that of J.E. Palmer, fishmonger. He was a trawler owner and fish, game and poultry salesman, with a delivery service so that 'customers can have their fish and poultry cleaned and sent to any part of the town'. A sight not often seen today are the rabbit and poultry seen hanging up outside the shop.

40. *Brothwell and Mills Ltd. 1912.* With their premises in Fletcher Street, Brothwell and Mills were a well established firm of mineral water manufacturers. Making, bottling and delivering such drinks as lemonade, soda water, ginger ale, hop bitters and thurstoh. The originaters of this firm came from Dronfield, in the 1880's, when that town removed with its steel works into Workington.

41. *Griffin Street, circa 1900.* This street was sited on the Cloffocks, which lies below the town. Running towards the River Derwent the Cloffocks have been regarded as Workington's playground. This open space has been the venue for the travelling fairs that have visited the area, and still is. Here today can be found the Greyhound Stadium and the local Football Ground. In the early years of this century one of the local characters was known as Paddy Whangs. More correctly he was Sgt. Wilson of the local Police Force who lived with his wife in Gladstone Street. He suffered with sore feet and off duty wore his boots well open. When called out to deal with any problems etc., people were always asked to wait a short while for him to fasten his 'whangs' (boot laces).

42. *Workington Jail or Lock up Shop.* Situated on Ritson Street just around the corner from Nook Street Police Station is this the Jailhouse. Erected in 1895 by public subscription, it carries a ground rent of 2 shillings 'for ever'. In its time it has held many a drunk and minor miscreants. The petty sessions were held in the Police Station on Nook Street.

43. *Guard Street, 1900.* The junction of Guard Street and Washington Street was the site of the Cattle Auction Market, now a garage. These three pigs strolling along Harrington Road, appear to be content to make their own way there.

44. *The High Market before 1900.* Workington's first market, sometimes called the Butter Market, was held in the upper part of the town at the junction of Curwen Street, Portland Street and Upper Jane Street. As the Market Place it was considered by 1901 to be too small to meet the requirements of the town so the open air market was removed to Hagg Hill. The covered market hall opened in 1861 and built on the site of the Old Slaughter House, held 21 stalls. Its main entrance was in Portland Street.

45. *The Central Hotel, Central Square, 1912.* The Central Hotel was established in the early 19th century as a posting house. As Workington's premier hotel it was the venue for dances, dinner parties and advertised itself in 1912 as having 'one of the finest and most luxurious dining halls in the North'. It further advertised itself as having coaches meet the trains but this must have applied to the Low Station as the Central Station was just across the road.

46. *Finkle Street about 1900.* This view of Finkle Street is looking down to South William Street. To the right, Listers, the house furnishers. This later was taken over by Piper's Penny Bazaar with the top floor being occupied by Charnley's Billard Saloon. Listers would appear to be advertising a retirement sale.

47. *The Beehive Co-operative Society on Vulcan's Lane 1912.* The Co-operative Society was established in Workington in 1865. Shoppers were members and shareholders. By quoting their sharenumber every time they made a purchase, the members would receive a dividend every six or twelve months. The dividend of 6 pence or possibly a shilling in the pound on their purchases, was based on the Society's profits. The Co-operative Society itself had four branches, and the Central Stores in Jane Street possessed a hall and suite of rooms let for dancing and supper parties. The Beehive Co-operative Society pictured here had its premises on Vulcan's Lane and as the photograph shows the row of shops included a grocers, greengrocers, shoe shop, etc. They also had eight branches.

48. *A dentist's surgery, 1912.* Mr. T. Thexton Smith was a local dentist and 'invites all who are interested in the care of their teeth to call at, 18 Nook Street, Workington'. He advertised himself with a little verse: *Even so small a thing as a tooth, has caused; Generals to lose Battles, Ministers to lose the threads of their discourse, Philosophers to cease philosophising, Poets to write drivel instead of Elegiacs.* The photograph shows the interior of the surgery and the tools of the trade.

49. *Ambrose Palmer, 1912.* Ambrose Palmer was the county painter and decorator. His large business was brought into being to 'supply the Country Gentry with that high standard of Work usually associated with London firms'.

50. *Portland Square, 1900.* Portland Square is situated in the upper part of the town and with its cobbled street and a surround of trees is a reminder of the old Workington. The Memorial in the centre of the square is to Dr. Anthony Peat, a local surgeon, who by his devotion to the medical profession did a lot to ease the suffering in the town. In the square were too the Assembly Rooms, where the various Friendly and Benovolent Societies met and flourished.

51. *Fisher Street, 1910.* Another of Workington's shopping areas, this time in the lower part of the town. Here are to be found in 1910, a grocers, Murdochs the piano and organ manufacturers and the Cash Boot Company among others.

52. *Workington Bridge, circa 1910.* The first stone bridge over the River Derwent was sited just below the Hall and was built in 1650, later replaced by another one in 1763. This was a somewhat dangerous structure and because of its narrowness was the scene of several accidents. So this present one of three arches was erected in 1841 to replace it.

53. *John Street, circa 1915.* This photograph shows the premises of J. Lindsay and Sons, wholesale grocers and butter and cheese purveyers. First established in 1881 they delivered their goods to the district shops by horse-drawn wagons and as the picture shows progressed to motor vans. Note the hams hung up in the doorway.

54. *Lindsay and Sons.* The town used to hold 'Shopping Weeks' during the twenties and thirties, with the various traders taking part in the Carnival Processions and displaying their wares. One year Lindsay and Sons, entered a horse and cart advertising flour, using full bags of flour. The amount and weight proved to be too much for the beast so at the last minute a second horse had to be found and the amount of flour reduced. The photograph shows them just before entering the carnival.

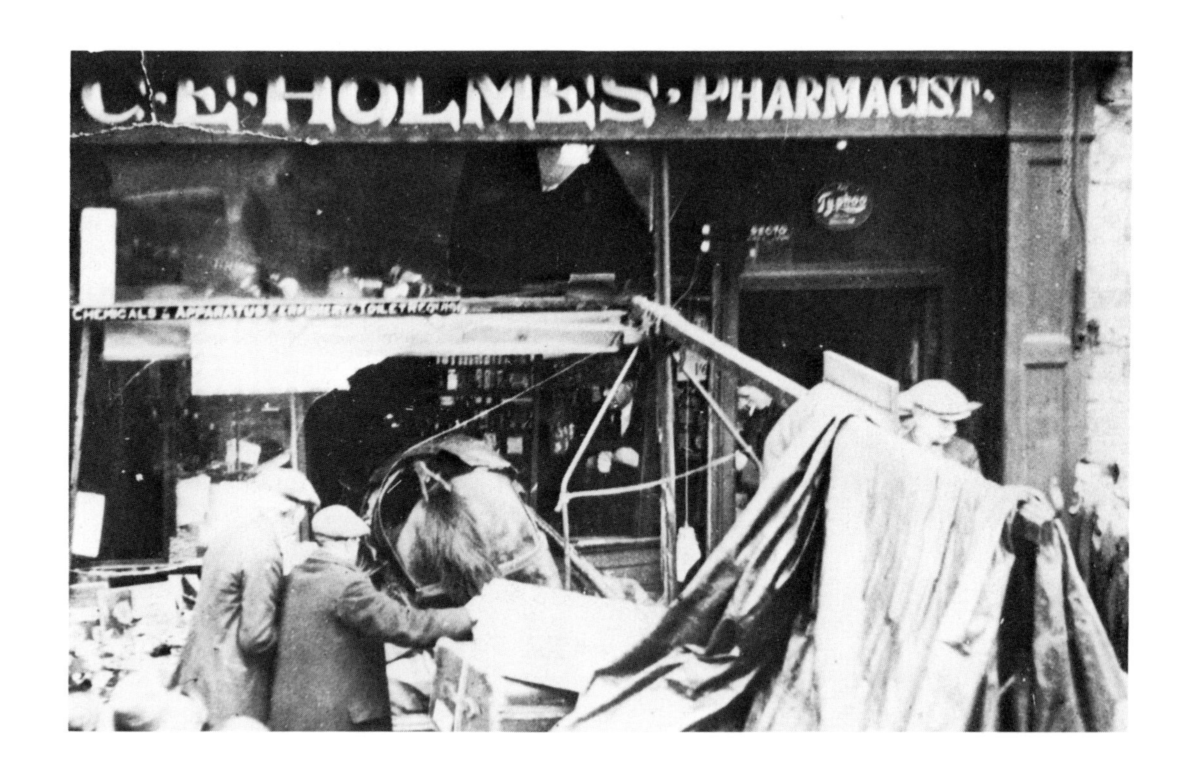

55. *A horse through a window.* Another incident in the life of Workington, for which unfortunately details are unknown, occurred some fifty-one years ago. A horse drawing a railway delivery cart on coming down the steep incline of Mason Street bolted and galloping through the junction with Harrington Road, went straight through the window of C.E. Holmes, the chemists. What damage was done, apart from that to the shop, is not known.

56. *The Uppies and Downies, 1910.* Annually at Easter, Workington holds this mass football game, the 'Uppies and Downies' contest. A traditional game its origins are lost. It quite possibly goes back to Saxon times and is a game in which there are no teams, the towns people in general taking part. The Uppies goal is the Hall Park in the upper part of the town, whilst the Downies attempt to score in the lower area of the town at Merchants Quay. The ball is centred on the Cloffocks, thrown, and then there are no holds barred as either side endeavours to 'hail' it at their respective end of the town. It is generally confined to the Cloffocks and up and down the river but can spill over into the town. Broken windows and arms or legs are not unknown.

57. *Curly Hill, 1908.* Curly Hill was a well-known character in those days and he took part regularly in the 'Uppies and Downies Games' as starter and player. He is pictured here with the ball in 1908. The ball although small is hand-stitched leather and stuffed with sawdust. In those days it was made by Mr. James Elwood, a saddler who had his shop on Nook Street.

58. *Windy Nooks Football Team, 1921*. Amateur football was a very popular sport especially amongst the steel and iron workers and miners. It had its regular leagues with cups and medals to be won. Seen above are the Windy Nooks Team of 1921 to 1922. All these men worked for the local iron and steel company and lived in the Moss Bay area of Derwent Crossings. Moss Bay Exchange, later Moss Bay Rangers, were another team from this same area.

59. *The Coal Strike of 1912.* Workington's success as an industrial town has been built partly on coal. In such places as Windscales Moor, about a mile or two out of town, coal can be found lying just beneath the surface of the fields. Coal also lies on the sea bed, to be washed ashore during gales or rough weather. This sea coal is regularly collected by the economically minded. During the Coal Strike of 1912 it was to these places and others such as the local Gas Works that the townspeople went to gather coal, taking and filling their own sacks, some of them even travelling long distances. The photograph shows children collecting coal from an outcrop near St. Michael's Road.

60. *The Tommies Organ Grinder Party, circa 1915.* The Tommies Organ Grinders were a fund raising group of entertainers during the First World War, organised by the teachers and pupils of Victoria School, Workington. They entertained on the streets and in the Concert Halls, raising money for comforts for the soldiers in the front line. They are seen here outside the Central Hotel.

61. *The Royal Visit, 1917.* The advent of the 1914-1918 War brought about a large amount of work for the iron and steel industry in Workington. It was a time for celebration therefore, when to mark the war effort, Moss Bay Works received a visit from King George and Queen Mary on 17th May 1917. The photograph shows the Royal couple arriving by car.

62. *The Coronation Arch, 1910.* Royal celebrations have always been a cause of rejoicing by the towns people of Workington. This triumphal arch was erected and stood at the end of Station Road as an entrance to the station. It was built in order to celebrate the coronation of Edward VII in 1901.

63. *The Co-op window display in 1910.* On Royal occasions the town enjoyed dressing up the streets and trading establishments produced highly colourful displays in the windows. This patriotic window display was done by the No. 1 branch of the Workington Cooperative Society to celebrate the accession of George V in 1910.

64. *The Orange Day Parade of 1931.* The Workington Lodge of the Loyal Order of Orangemen, has long been a feature of Workington life. Here they are seen just before one of their parades in 1931.

65. *The Salvation Army.* The Workington Corps of the Salvation Army commenced their activities in October 1886 in what was the 875th corps to be opened. Success and opposition to this new religion both marked those early days. Crowds attended the meetings, many were converted and eventually a band was formed. Open air meetings were not looked upon with favour and on occasions Salvationists were summonsed for holding open meetings in North Watt Street. Unwilling to pay the fine, officers elected to go to jail and on their release, processions were formed in which the ex-prisoners rode in a wagonette followed by great crowds rejoicing. The Army's meetings were held in Albert Hall and a little hall behind a Pow Street shop. During 1922 and 1923, when a great number of converts were secured, the Carnegie Hall was filled every Sunday night. Eventually the corps took over the Citadel in Edkin Street. The photograph shows a meeting at the Citadel in 1923.

66. *The Beach at Long and Smalls.* Up the coast from Workington is the village of Flimby. Here at a stretch of beach known locally as Long and Smalls was the leisure area for summer picnics. Sunny weekends of the 1920's and 1930's quite often saw this grassy shore being enjoyed by cyclists and picnickers alike.

67. *Vulcan's Park, circa 1928.* Situated in the town is this leisure area. In keeping with all Municipal Parks, it has a childrens play area, rose and flower gardens and in addition to tennis courts there is a Crazy Golf Course. Workington's Memorial to the war dead was unveiled on 24th June 1928.

68. *The Bread and Beer House, circa 1910.* In addition to inns and hotels, Workington had a few beer houses. This one was sited on Whitehaven Road. Belonging to the nearby farm it dispensed refreshments to Sunday strollers out enjoying the countryside. As its name suggests it sold more than just alcoholic beverages.

69. *Workington bus station circa 1928.* Workington bus station as a member of the Cumberland Motor Service was opened on 19th March 1926. The opening ceremony was performed by Alderman Baines. The depot was erected to contain fifty buses which offer a service all over north-west Cumbria.

70. *Harrington Road Cemetery, 1910.* There were two cemeteries adjoining the town. The Bank Cemetery for Catholics, and this the Harrington Road Cemetery. The portion that was set apart for members of the Anglican Church was consecrated by the Bishop of Carlisle and the first person to be interred there on 19th February 1879 was the late Charles Litt Esq. of Stainburn. Owing to the free ground in Bank Cemetery being filled a section of Harrington Road Cemetery was set aside for the use of Catholics.

71. *Jane Pit, circa 1890.* Coal mining activities have long been part of the Workington scene. In the 19th century there were many one seam pits employing no more than twenty miners. The town is built on some of these pits. Vulcan's Park, the Technical College and John Street are all sited on former pits. The areas of Westfield and Moorbanks had about six at various times during the 1800's. The photograph shows Jane Pit at Westfield, 1843 to 1875, with its castellated style and turreted chimney. A monument to Workington's past that still stands today.

72. *Shipbuilders yards, Workington.* Messrs R. Williamson & Son, who for many years carried on the business of building wooden ships at Harrington removed to Workington and began iron and steel shipbuilding in 1881. The firm employed about 150 people. Named the 'Sodality' the last and 244th ship was launched in 1938.

73. *Moss Bay Iron Works circa 1920.* Workington's main industry for the past hundred years has been that of steel making. Moss Bay Iron Works originated when Messrs. Kirk and Valentine leased some land down by the shore in July 1872. On this site were erected blast furnaces for the production of pig iron. 1887 saw the addition of a bessemer steel making plant and the company rolled their first rails on 13th August 1887.

74. *Pouring blast furnace slag, circa 1910.* The Moss Bay Company had its good and bad times. There were formations of two new companies due to under financing and losses of the original company. The board of the new company installed new equipment including the then wonder of the age, electricity. Plant breakdowns were only too frequent however, and in 1882 the mills were idle for a number of months. In 1883, trade slackened and the workforce had to take a reduction of ten percent on their wages. This resulted in a lengthy strike. The following years saw similar disruptions until in 1909 the company amalgamated with the other iron making companies in the local area to form the Workington Iron Company. The photograph shows the pouring of 'slag'. This is the residue left after the molten iron has been drawn off.

75. *Derwent blast furnaces, circa 1910.* The Derwent Works started operations on the site adjacent to the Moss Bay Works in 1873 under the title of the Derwent Hematite Iron Company, with the building of the first blast furnace in 1874 followed by another two by 1879. Around this period had been developing another industrial story which was to have great repercussions for Workington. In Dronfield, in Yorkshire, Charles Cammell and Company in 1870, opened a mill to make iron wheels and later added a bessemer converter to make steel and a rail mill to make railway lines. Access to shipping and raw materials were a costly problem for the company. Workington had none of these disadvantages. In addition to ore mines in the vicinity and local coal mines, Derwent Works had a direct line to Workington Docks.

76. *Charles Cammell and Company, circa 1900.* In August 1882, Charles Cammell bought the Derwent Works and in April 1883 the Dronfield Works were transported to Workington and erected on the Derwent site. With the works came the workforce together with a number of Dronfield traders and shopkeepers. Today, many a Workingtonian can lay claim to a 'Dronie' ancestry. The town of Dronfield died. The locals did not at first take to this invasion of 'foreigners' and fights between Dronies and locals occurred, until the towns people eventually came to terms with the outsiders.

77. *The casting crane in the bessemer shop, 1910.* Once settled in Workington, Charles Cammell and Co., added to their empire with the Harrington Iron Works and collieries, ore mines and a part interest in Workington Dock, and Harrington harbour. In 1909 they proposed the amalgamation with Moss Bay Works to form the Workington Iron and Steel Company.

78. *A group of steel workers from 1914.* The First World War brought a heavy demand for steel and full employment after a period of indifferent trade. 800 men off to War, was met by the employment of women. Open hearth furnaces were installed to augment the supply of shell steel and German prisoners of war were employed on the building of these furnaces.

79. *The Royal visit to Moss Bay in 1917.* In order to celebrate Workington's achievements and increased trade, the town received a visit from their Majesties, King George V and Queen Mary on 17th May 1917. The Royal couple arrived in Moss Bay and toured the works.

80. *Projectile loaders. Some of the Iron Works Workforce of 1920.* The early 1920's after the war were difficult times. Trade depression and a 14 week coal strike in 1921 saw the works being closed for 23 weeks with only intermittent working afterwards. The blast furnaces of Harrington, Solway, Lowther, Distington and Oldside were closed down and eventually demolished.

81. *Workington illuminations, circa 1920.* 1929 was notable for large tonnages of rails to Argentina, but this was followed by a world wide depression. The company had a hard time and it was not until a tariff of 30 percent was imposed on imported steel in 1932, that trade improved. The photograph shows a sight that will never be seen again: the glow from the furnaces at night. The steel company were eventually nationalised under British Steel and in 1974 the making of steel was abandoned. All that is left of these two companies are the Rail Rolling Mills, shaping railway lines from imported steel.

82. *Harrington Works, 1912.* These works started up in 1857, with just one furnace and eventually four. The location of the works was ideal because of its proximity to the Whitehaven Junction Railway and the link with the Cleator Railway bringing ore direct from the ore mines in the Egremont areas. It was also sited next to the Harrington Dock for the shipping out of iron made. The works closed in 1926.

83. *Distington explosion, 1909.* Distington Iron Company, 1878 to 1922, was one of the smaller works near Workington, which in 1919 became one of the United Steel Companies. It is more likely remembered for the disaster that occurred on 18th September 1909, when four of a set of eleven boilers were blown into pieces. Two boiler halves landed in a field about a quarter of a mile away. No one was killed or even injured in the blast.

84. *The rail rolling mills, 1912.* Since 1896, Workington Steel Works have been making and exporting railway lines to all parts of the world. Texas, South America, Australia and New Zealand, just to mention a few. The photograph shows the interior of the rolling mill.

85. *Oldside and Lowther Iron Works. Circa 1910.* It was in 1856 that the Workington Heamatite Company first built their furnaces at Oldside on the north side of the harbour. These works were to cease operations in 1930. The Lowther Iron Works had already ceased working in 1911. The photograph shows the harbour and in the distance these two works.

86. *Prince of Wales Dock about 1925.* The widening and deepening of the harbour led to the erection of the Prince of Wales Dock. Work commencing on 22nd November 1922 and completed in June 1927. Using a pair of golden scissors to cut the ribbon the Prince of Wales declared the dock open on 30th June 1927. The photograph was taken sometime during the improvements.

87. *The workforce of Ogden and Lawsons, 1913.* The firm of Ogden and Lawson, makers of brass industrial artifacts, were established in the late 19th century and had their premises in Stanley Street. The photograph shows the workmen and boys of 1913.

88. *Workington Bridge and Boiler Company.* These works were situated on the Marsh Side. They carried on an extensive business in the construction and erection of blast furnace and steel works plant, bridgework, iron and steel rivets and railway spikes etc. In 1901 they were turning out a hundred tons weekly.

89. *Pow Street in the 1890's.* Looking down towards Finkle Street the gable end is the Appletree Inn and also to the left can be seen the railway bridge.

90. *Marsh and Quay in the 1920's.* Situated down by the harbour the Marsh and Quay was mainly occupied by fishermen and dock workers. In this district were also sited the shipyards, the roperies and brass and iron foundries.

91. *The Soapery, 1910.* The Soapery lies down Hall Brow and just before the turn to cross Workington Bridge. Its name is derived from the local term for the old laundry which was sited here in the 19th century.

92. *Jubilee Celebrations in 1897.* During the Diamond Jubilee of Queen Victoria in 1897 the town celebrated in style. Here the Workington Men's Conservative Club dressed the premises of the Central Square building in flags and bunting.

93. *Ladies of the Co-op in 1916.* Workington had two Co-operative Societies. The Beehive Co-operative Society with its headquarters in Vulcan's Lane and the Workington Co-operative Society who had a central stores in Jane Street. Here we have the staff of the ladies department of the Jane Street store on Empire Day 1916.

94. *Ellis Sports Ground 1925.* Workington Rugby Union Football Club or the Workington 'Zebras' were the County Cup Winners in 1923-24. In 1925 they were granted the Home Ground of Ellis Sport Field in September 1925. The photograph shows the opening match. Their opponents were a team brought in by R. Oaks, the then Yorkshire President and England Rugby Union Selector.

95. *Freddie Cairns, circa 1925.* Freddie Cairns was one of the town's well-loved characters during the early years of this century. He was the local rag and bone man. With his cry of 'gather up your rags and bones' he toured the streets collecting rags and giving in exchange his home-made windmills.

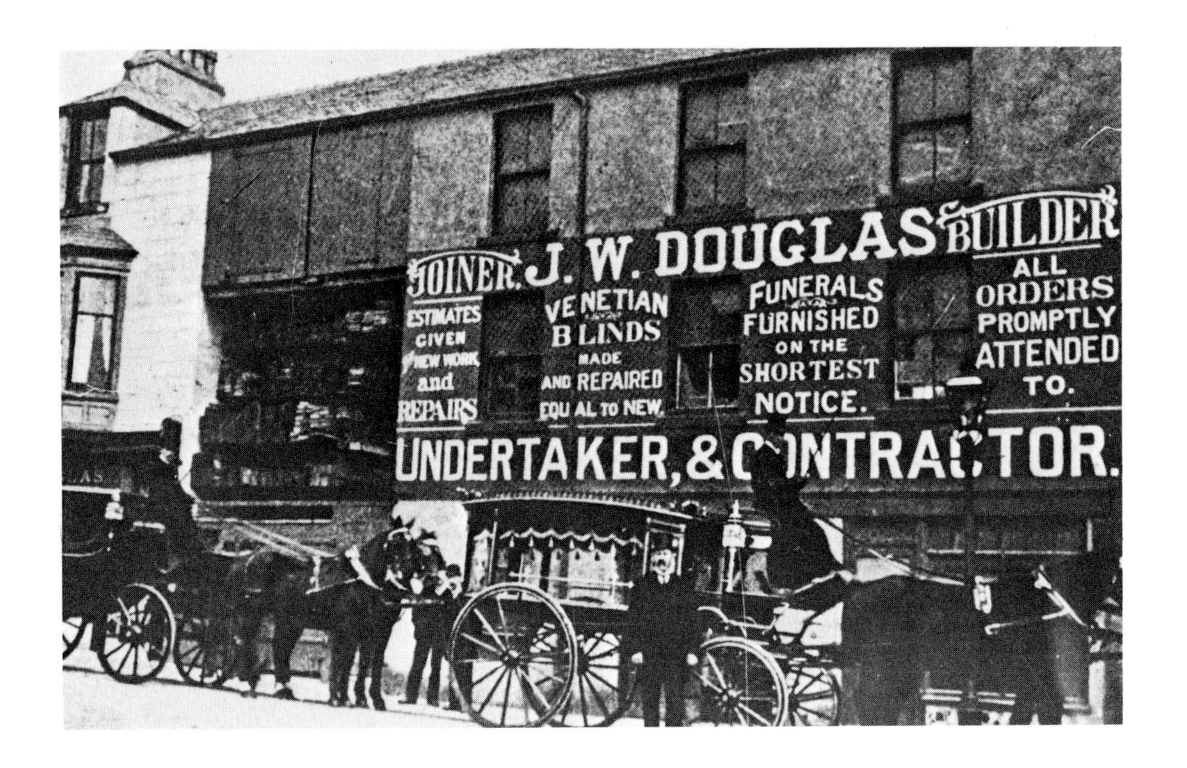

96. *John Street, 1912.* One of the businesses on John Street in 1912, was that of Douglas the undertaker and joiner. He kept an excellent team of horses and although a sad sight, his horse-drawn cortege was very impressive.

97. *Washington Street, circa 1920.* This is the western side of Washington Street showing the hotels of The Old Crown and on the opposite corner the New Crown. Next door to the Old Crown on the left is Gordon's the garage and to the right of the New Crown was a sweets and confectioners shop (Varty's).

98. *Upper Jane Street about 1915.* This view is looking down Upper Jane Street to Jane Street and beyond to Central Square with Oxford Street in the distance. To the right was the chemist shop of Herbert Smith. In 1912, Seven Oils (the best rub for rhumatism, lumbago, etc.) sold for a shilling a bottle, and 'Corn Charm, really did kill Corns for 7½d a bottle'. To quote his advertisement.

99. *Pow Street, circa 1910.* This is the central area of Pow Street. Note the summer outfits of the ladies. To the right can be seen an old gas lamp. The gasworks were established in Workington by a private company in 1840 and then taken over by the town seven years later.

100. *Stainburn Hall, 1900.* Stainburn is a village and out township about a mile eastwards of Workington on the Cockermouth Road. The Earl of Lonsdale was the Lord of the Manor and owned about half the land. In addition to a Board School, there were several fine residences including this of Stainburn Hall, which in the 1900's belonged to the Harrison's.

101. *Church Road, Harrington, 1900.* The town and port of Harrington lie just south of Workington. The parish extends two miles and a half along the coast and about one mile inland. A hundred years ago it was a town of well-built houses, a fine harbour covering two-and-a-half acres and with a quay, attending to a very large number of shipping vessels. The photograph shows the main thoroughfare of Church Road, with its shops and school. Note the fishermen with their catches.

102. *Harrington harbour, circa 1910.* The harbour was the property of the Curwens of Workington, but the lessees were the Harrington Harbour Board, representing Charles Cammell and Co., the Moss Bay Iron and Steel Co., and James Bain and Co. The coal trade which is chiefly with Ireland gives a large trade to a number of vessels. Lime was quarried in Distington and exported to Scotland or used in the blast furnaces of Harrington Iron Works.

103. *Harrington dock and quayside, mid-1920's.* The harbour which was extended and altered in about 1890 was for an increasing number of vessels. Ships registered to the port in 1822 were 38. In 1828 this was increased to 43, with a carrying capacity equal to 5,479 tons. By 1840 there were 44 vessels registered to the port. During 1899, 755 steamers discharged and loaded at this port. Pig iron from the Harrington furnaces was also an export.

104. *Copperas Hill Railway Station, circa 1930.* Coal was abundant in the parish, giving employment to a large number of the population. Although the colliery at one time consisted of nine pits by 1901 only three remained. These pits extended about a mile under the sea. The coal was transported to the harbour by this mineral railway which also ran to the collieries at Lowca. The station stands at the head of an incline leading down to the harbour. At times two engines were required to haul the wagons. Break away wagons carreering down the incline and straight into the harbour did occur, luckily with very few fatalities.

105. *The quayside at Harrington, circa 1925.* This was the area of harbourside shops, with Deans the newsagent very prominent. Far right and bottom of the picture can be seen the lines of the Harrington and Lowca Light Railway, down which would come the wagons from Copperas Hill.

106. *Rose Hill, Harrington, circa 1880.* Rose Hill stands on an eminence overlooking Harrington itself. From here is an excellent view of the harbour and out to sea. The hill which is a street of houses was inhabited by Master Mariners, Stevedores and the like, families with maritime connections etc. The photograph shows such a family who resided there in the late 19th century.

107. *High Harrington Station, circa 1925.* High Harrington is a community that runs from Harrington itself towards Whitehaven. At one time it possessed its own railway station, as a halt on the Workington to Cleator Moor Line. This line was opened in 1875 as a mineral line, then taking eventual passengers.

108. *Scaw Road gravestone.* On Scaw Road, High Harrington one can find a gravestone by the side of the road hedge. Back in the 18th century a certain Mr. Thompson had a diseased thumb which made amputation necessary. His requirements were to have the thumb buried in a grave to which he would, in the fullness of time go to himself. The local vicar would have none of this. There then followed a very strong argument, with Mr. Thompson (a pillar of the Church), refusing to be buried in the church altogether and breaking with the church. When Mr. Thompson eventually died he was buried in one of the fields of High Harrington. His gravestone was later moved to its present position during the making of Scaw Road.

109. *Beach Scene, Harrington, circa 1930.* The prosperity of Harrington was also dependent upon the iron works. This trade commenced in 1857, finally closing its gates in 1926. Consisting of four furnaces turning out pig iron, they employed about 250 men. Despite the presence of the iron works the beach was a popular resort for bathers as the above photograph shows.

110. *Victoria Square, Harrington, circa 1925.* The Manor of Harrington was granted after the Conquest to the family of de Talbois, who held it as a fee of Workington. It was possessed by several Harringtons of which there were many branches of the family, until the estates became the property of one Thomas Grey, Lord of Dorset. It was his grandson, who created Duke of Suffolk attempted to put upon the throne of England his daughter, the lady Jane Grey. Together with his daughter he was beheaded by the orders of Mary Tudor. The Manor passed to the Crown and then to the Curwens. The rooms of the Victoria buildings shown in the photograph housed the Literary Association and also the Salvation Army.

111. *Harrington Church, 1912.* The church occupies a nice situation overlooking the town and a 12th century font is to be found in the porch. The church would appear to have been in existance as early as the Norman period and at one point during the rebuilding of 1885 a Roman alter was discovered, which is now in the Museum at Newcastle. The church consists of nave and chancel, with a square tower, which in 1901 held a bell dated 1670.

112. *Harrington Infants School, class of 1930.* The School Board was formed in December 1873. There were three schools. The Senior Mixed, built on an eminence above Church Road in 1897. (Now Harrington Juniors.) The Junior Mixed, erected in 1875 (Harrington Infants), and the Lowca School which held a small number of pupils only. Also on Church Road was the Catholic School of St. Mary's.

113. *Harrington Mill, circa 1920.* Harrington, like Workington, had its own corn mill. Situated in farmland just above the village it was unusual in that, whilst being operated by a water wheel, the wheel was supplied with water via an overhead mill race. Water was carried by means of an overhead chute.

114. *Seaton Mill, about 1910.* Seaton Mill was also used for the grinding of corn, etc. Like Harrington it too was unusual with its overhead water chute. In 1852, while digging around the foundations as part of a drainage scheme, workmen discovered some Roman altars, one of which was preserved in the mill garden. On a nearby hill were also found human skeletons and a number of animal horns and bones.

115. *Camerton Church, circa 1900.* The church occupies a situation in a loop of the River Derwent. It is said to have been first erected in 1000, rebuilt in 1694 and again in 1796. Until St. Michael's received the right to interment, all local burials were conducted here. In the church is the effigy of a Knight in Black Marble, 'Black Tom of the North'. Tradition has it that it is Thomas de Culwen, ancestor of the Curwen family and a renowned warrior of his day. Thomas, son of Gospatric, by marriage with the heiress of Culwen brought the name of Curwen into the family. Involved in the Border Wars against the Scots he lies buried in Shap Abbey.

116. *Clifton Village, 1912.* Originally called Kirk Clifton, the village lies on the south side of the River Derwent, on the Cockermouth Road. Although a farming community, coal was worked at the William Pit. Owned by the Allerdale Coal Company it employed about 350.